W9-BPS-090

Steve Austin
The Story of the Wrestler
They Call "Stone Cold"

Chyna

Mick Foley
The Story of the Wrestler
They Call "Mankind"

Ric Flair
The Story of the Wrestler
They Call "The Nature Boy"

Bill Goldberg

Billy Kidman

Brett Hart
The Story of the Wrestler
They Call "The Hitman"

The Story of the Wrestler
They Call "Hollywood"
Hulk Hogan

Lex Luger
The Story of the Wrestler
They Call "The Total Package"

Shawn Michaels
The Story of the Wrestler
They Call "The Heartbreak Kid"

Vince McMahon Jr.

Kevin Nash

The Story of the Wrestler
They Call "Diamond"
Dallas Page

Pro Wrestling: The Early Years

Pro Wrestling's
Greatest Tag Teams

Pro Wrestling's
Greatest Matches

Pro Wrestling's Greatest Wars

Pro Wrestling's Most
Punishing Finishing Moves

The Story of the Wrestler
They Call "The Rock"

Randy Savage
They Story of the Wrestler
They Call "Macho Man"

They Story of the Wrestler
They Call "Sting"

They Story of the Wrestler
They Call "The Undertaker"

Jesse Ventura
They Story of the Wrestler
They Call "The Body"

The Women of Pro Wrestling

CHELSEA HOUSE PUBLISHERS

Randy Savage
The Story of the Wrestler
They Call "Macho Man"

Jacqueline Mudge

Chelsea House Publishers
Philadelphia

Produced by Choptank Syndicate, Inc.

Editor and Picture Researcher: Mary Hull
Design and Production: Lisa Hochstein

CHELSEA HOUSE PUBLISHERS

Editor in Chief: Stephen Reginald
Managing Editor: James D. Gallagher
Production Manager: Pamela Loos
Art Director: Sara Davis
Director of Photography: Judy L. Hasday
Senior Production Editor: LeeAnne Gelletly
Cover Illustrator: Keith Trego

Cover Photos: WCW
　　　　　　　Jeff Eisenberg Sports Photography

The Chelsea House World Wide Web site
address is http://www.chelseahouse.com

　3　5　7　9　8　6　4

Library of Congress Cataloging-in-Publication Data

Mudge, Jacqueline
　　Randy Savage: the story of the wrestler they call "Macho Man" / Jacqueline Mudge.
　　　　p.　cm.　— (Pro wrestling legends)
　　Includes bibliographical references (p.　) and index.
　　Summary: A biography of the professional wrestler who has won—and lost—both
the World Wrestling Federation and World Championship Wrestling titles.
　　ISBN 0-7910-5409-8 (hard.) — ISBN 0-7910-5555-8 (pbk.)
　　1. Savage, Randy—Juvenile literature. 2. Wrestlers—United States—Biography—
Juvenile literature. [1. Savage, Randy. 2. Wrestlers.]
I. Title. II. Series.
GV1196.S38M84　1999
796.812'092—dc21
[B]　　　　　　　　　　　　　　　　　　　　　　　　　　　　　99-33772
　　　　　　　　　　　　　　　　　　　　　　　　　　　　　　　　　CIP

Contents

1 REVENGE IS SWEET

Sometimes people wrestle for glory. Sometimes they wrestle for money. Sometimes they wrestle because they like seeing their names in lights. Sometimes they wrestle for the pure love of the sport. Sometimes it's simply just a matter of revenge.

And once in a great while, a man wrestles for love, honor, and pride.

The months leading up to WrestleMania VIII were a living nightmare for Randy Savage. His marriage to Elizabeth—his manager, partner, and friend—was falling apart after only a year and a half. To make matters worse, people were talking about the "Macho Man," and what they were saying wasn't kind. The word around wrestling was that Savage was washed up. His career, people were saying loud and often, was over.

Savage had been on top of the world just a few years earlier, on March 27, 1988. That was when he won his first World Wrestling Federation (WWF) World championship at WrestleMania IV. He didn't stay at the top for long, though: only a year later, he lost the World championship to Hulk Hogan at WrestleMania V.

How far had Savage fallen since then?

Randy Savage attends a press conference with his manager Elizabeth after winning his first WWF World championship at Wrestlemania IV on March 27, 1988.

Jake "the Snake" Roberts was one of Savage's staunchest foes in the WWF.

At WrestleMania VI, he wrestled in a mixed tag team match: Savage and Sherri Martel against Dusty Rhodes and Sapphire. The bout was widely considered to be one of the most embarrassing matches of this installment of the annual WrestleMania extravaganza.

At WrestleMania VII, he lost a loser-must-retire match to the Ultimate Warrior.

A poisonous snake bite in 1991 nearly took his life.

The WWF reinstated Savage by popular acclaim, shortly after his marriage to Elizabeth, but he didn't return to the ring with any major significance. Thirsting for revenge against his foe Jake "the Snake" Roberts, he slumped badly and embarked on an uncharacteristic losing streak.

Just four years after Savage had won the World championship, "Machomania" was dead.

The course of events that placed Savage's career back on the right track began on December 4, 1991, and had absolutely nothing to do with Savage. That day, WWF President Jack Tunney declared the World championship vacant. Tunney also announced that the title vacancy would be filled by the winner of the federation's annual Royal Rumble, to be held January 19, 1992.

Tunney was sharply criticized for his decision. A lot of wrestling purists felt a major world championship shouldn't be put up for grabs in what was, in effect, a 30-man battle royal. But just about every wrestler in the WWF saw it as a golden opportunity, a once-in-a-lifetime chance to become World champion.

For Savage, it was a chance to instantly revitalize his career. He came close to succeeding. Savage, Ric Flair, Sid Justice, and Hulk Hogan were the last four men remaining in the ring when Flair combined with Justice to dump Savage over the top rope to the arena floor, eliminating him. Just a few minutes later, Flair won his first WWF World championship. And he wasted no time setting his sights on Savage. Or, more specifically, on the lovely Elizabeth.

In a fabulous career that spanned three decades, Flair had established himself as one of the greatest wrestlers ever. But he had also established himself as a ruthless, egotistical individual who wanted to destroy his opponents physically and emotionally.

An article in the August 1992 issue of *Inside Wrestling* magazine spelled out Flair's cruel game plan to antagonize his foes. Flair would steal his opponent's girlfriend the night before their match, then make sure his opponents found out about it.

This was exactly the game plan Flair used on Savage after it was announced that the Macho Man would wrestle the "Nature Boy" at WrestleMania VIII. Savage had embarked on a fierce winning streak after the Royal Rumble, destroying every opponent in his path and regaining the killer instinct that had made him great in the first place. Flair should have known better than to aggravate Savage more than necessary. Curt Hennig, Flair's closest adviser at the time, warned Flair against picking on Elizabeth, knowing how much she meant to Savage. Stoking Savage's rage, Hennig knew, would be a fatal mistake for Flair.

Flair ignored him.

"Elizabeth was mine before she was yours," Flair told Savage during the weeks prior to WrestleMania. He claimed to have photographs of himself and Elizabeth on dates. Then he claimed to have dumped her. A few weeks before WrestleMania, Flair produced the incriminating photographs of him and Elizabeth. Many people suspected the photographs had been doctored.

Whether the photographs were faked or not didn't matter to Savage. He was as mad as a man could be.

This unusual series of events, almost like something out of an afternoon television soap opera, set the stage for the main event. Savage wanted the World Championship, that's for sure. But more than anything else, he wanted to destroy Flair for what he had been saying. This match was about glory, and certainly it was about money, but it was mostly about revenge and pride.

Savage couldn't wait to get his hands on Flair, and he didn't wait. The crowd of 62,167 that turned out for the World Championship match at the Hoosier Dome in Indianapolis, Indiana, didn't even have time to sit down after the prematch introductions when Savage brutally assaulted Flair outside the ring. He attacked with the blind fury of a man who has been insulted too many times, relentlessly

Ric Flair became Savage's archenemy when he tried to steal Elizabeth away from the Macho Man.

banging Flair's head into the floor. It required
the interference of Hennig, Flair's executive
assistant, to save the Nature Boy from a merci-
less beating.

The action returned to the ring, and Savage
continued his all-out attack. He clotheslined
Flair, then kneed him into the turnbuckle.
Flair actually gained control of the match and
outwrestled Savage for the next eight minutes,
even scoring a near-pin, but the Macho Man
would not be denied. He caught the champion
with a backdrop and two clotheslines, then
a reverse neckbreaker, in which the victim is
painfully thrown to the mat neck-first. Flair
begged for mercy. He was asking the wrong
man.

Savage again grabbed the Nature Boy by
the neck and sent him careening into the turnbuckle. Flair struck the turnbuckle with a
sickening thud, then grabbed his back in pain.
Flair leaped off the opposite turnbuckle, but
Savage caught him with a clothesline—a stiff
forearm against the neck. The action spilled
outside of the ring and Savage suplexed Flair
by placing him in a headlock, and lifting and
flipping him over his back onto the arena floor.
Then Savage banged Flair's head into the steel
ringsteps and ringpost.

Savage wasn't wrestling like a man who
wanted to be World champion, he was wrestling
like a man possessed. He was wrestling like a
man who wanted to right a horrible wrong, like
a man who had identified his worst enemy, and
now wanted to end his career. He wrestled like
a beast, not like a man, and only one question
remained: would Savage interrupt the beating
long enough to pin Flair?

When Hennig handed Flair a foreign object, Elizabeth ran to ringside to aid Savage. Several WWF officials tried to stop her, but nothing could prevent her from helping the Macho Man. Flair trapped Savage in a figure-four leglock, a submission hold in which the perpetrator locks his legs with one of his opponent's legs, putting incredible pressure on the victim's thigh muscles. No wrestler has ever applied the figure-four with greater efficiency than Flair; it is his signature move and has resulted in hundreds—perhaps thousands—of victories over the years.

Savage, however, wasn't just any opponent. He reversed the hold and nearly turned it into a pin of his own. Flair kicked out and got back to his feet.

The next 10 seconds appeared to move in slow motion. Flair reared back and prepared to deliver a big right hand. Savage didn't duck. Instead, he reacted and blocked the punch with his left hand. The crowd rose to its feet. Savage grabbed Flair's trunks with his right hand and pulled him to the mat. He covered him for the pin. The referee moved in to make the count. One! Two! Three! Revenge was Savage's!

The crowd exploded with excitement. Elizabeth, jubilant, ran into the ring to congratulate Savage. Flair, however, wasn't through with his insults. He got up, grabbed Elizabeth, and kissed her on the lips. The fans screamed with glee when Elizabeth slapped the Nature Boy across the face—and screamed even louder when Savage once again attacked Flair.

It was an amazing evening, the kind that people who love wrestling can never forget. For Savage and Elizabeth, it was a night to cherish.

2

"HE WRESTLED LIKE
A SAVAGE"

A ngelo Poffo was an outstanding high-flying wrestler in the 1940s, '50s, and '60s who prided himself on being in tremendous physical condition. For a while, he was famous for performing 6,033 consecutive situps, then a world record. But there came a time when Angelo Poffo became better known for something else: being the father of Randy "Macho Man" Savage.

Randy Savage was born Randy Poffo on November 15, 1952, in Columbus, Ohio, to Angelo and Judy Poffo, the former Judy Sverdlin. Randy's family moved to Downers Grove, Illinois, when he was young, and to this day he considers it his hometown. Two years after Randy came into the world, Angelo and Judy had another son, Lanny. One day, Lanny, too, would become a professional wrestler.

Growing up, Randy and Lanny frequently attended their father's matches. Although Angelo was known as a rule-breaker in the ring, he carefully taught his sons the basics of the sport. He thought it was important that they become good amateur wrestlers before they tried to make a living in the pro ranks. Randy and Lanny often wrestled together, and Angelo guided them in the scientific fundamentals and helped them

Randy Poffo, shown with his father, the legendary wrestler Angelo Poffo, in 1974, played minor league baseball for five years before turning to professional wrestling.

blend their natural athletic skills with hard lessons about the pro sport.

Randy was a natural athlete. He played all sports, but excelled in baseball and played on the Downers Grove North High School team. Randy hit over .500 in high school baseball and never lost track of his schoolwork. He was an excellent student and was named to the National Honor Society.

"That's as cool as being WWF champion," he would one day tell the *Chicago Tribune*. "I was, and still am, a goal-oriented person. I think that's very important, something that's helped me in school and sports."

Randy graduated from Downers Grove North in 1971 and decided he wanted to become a major league baseball player, just like his hero, Cincinnati Reds catcher Johnny Bench. He got a tryout with the St. Louis Cardinals, and soon afterward signed a minor league contract.

Randy started out as a catcher with the Orangeburg Cardinals of the Western Carolinas League under manager Jimmy Piersall (who many people remember from the movie *Fear Strikes Out*). Randy would spend five years in the minor leagues, playing for the Cardinals, Cincinnati Reds, and Chicago White Sox as a catcher and a first baseman. He once hit .350 for a rookie league team in Sarasota, Florida. Randy had an unusual distinction: not only was he a switch-hitter, which meant he could hit from both sides of the plate, but he was also a switch-thrower, which meant he could throw with either hand!

That distinction, however, wasn't enough to get Randy his big break in the major leagues. In

fact, he would never play in a major league game. Perhaps he realized that early on, because during his minor league career, he developed a longing to step into the pro wrestling ring. Because of his baseball contractual obligations, however, Randy was prohibited from playing any other pro sports. So, goal-oriented as he was, Randy donned a mask during the off-season, so that nobody would know who he was, and wrestled as the Spider.

In November 1973, at the age of 21, Randy made his pro debut as the Spider and beat Paul Christy in Clenbard, Illinois. He continued to wrestle as the Spider for three years, but balancing his baseball and wrestling careers was difficult. Wrestlers generally want to be as big and muscular as possible, but Randy had to keep his weight down to 175 pounds for baseball. He certainly couldn't show up for spring training weighing 210 pounds, then

Randy Poffo, far right, poses with teammates from the Tampa Tarpons, a Cincinnati Reds minor league team in 1974.

Randy's career took off after he signed with Mid-South wrestling in 1983 and began wrestling fan-favorite Jerry Lawler in front of sellout crowds.

hope to work the weight off; that would have been his instant one-way ticket out of baseball. But at 175 pounds, he had a lot of trouble contending with heavyweight wrestlers. Juggling baseball and wrestling became too difficult for Randy, who found it hard to get up in time for his morning baseball practice. According to his 1974 Tampa Tarpons teammate Joel Youngblood, Randy was chronically late for morning practice. One morning, the coach locked him off the field. "All of a sudden,"

Youngblood recalled, "you heard somebody yelling and come running up there full tilt to hit that gate. It was Randy. He had gotten a running start and jumped up on the gate and was just hanging there. Then he started climbing and he kind of just flipped himself over the top and came into practice like nothing was wrong. That was the funniest thing." Even then, Randy showed a streak of the madness and determination that would one day help him excel at pro wrestling.

The strain and stress of both careers was too much for Randy to bear for long. Although he was competent at baseball and wrestling, he was excelling at neither. Finally, he decided that his career prospects were better in the ring. In 1976 he stopped playing baseball, pulled off his mask, and devoted himself to a full-time wrestling career. He started out with his given name, Randy Poffo.

Randy wrestled throughout Georgia and Florida, which at the time had extremely competitive wrestling circuits. In fact, the Florida state heavyweight title and the Georgia National heavyweight title were, aside from the world titles, among the most sought-after championships in the sport. While in Georgia in 1976, Randy wrestled Ole Anderson, a legendary brawling wrestler who also came from a large wrestling family. Anderson was impressed by Randy's tenacity and killer instinct.

"He wrestled like a savage!" Ole exclaimed.

From that point on, Randy Poffo was known as Randy Savage.

Soon afterward, Randy left Georgia to wrestle in the Southeast area. He teamed with his brother, Lanny, and they won the Southeastern tag team championship. Randy and Lanny held the title for a few months before losing it and then went their separate ways.

The first half of Randy's career could aptly be titled, "Fourteen Years of Frustration." In the smaller federations, he had a reputation as a talented, hardworking wrestler, but the millions of fans who watched the big three federations—then the WWF, the National Wrestling Alliance (NWA), and the American Wrestling Association (AWA)—had never heard of him. Lanny, in fact, was the one who seemed destined for greater things when he won the International Championship Wrestling (ICW) heavyweight title in 1978. The ICW was owned by Randy and Lanny's father. At the time, it was the only federation that would have them.

Randy and Lanny didn't feud, but Randy did beat Lanny for the ICW title on July 21, 1979. He successfully defended the title for four years, which sounds like a much more impressive accomplishment than it actually was. Randy's career had stalled in the ICW. He was going nowhere fast. In fact, some people might have said he was going backwards. Randy lost the title in 1983 to Paul Christy, the same man he had beaten in his debut match 10 years earlier.

Randy was on the verge of failing in wrestling, just as he had failed in baseball, when he got his first big break: in late 1983, he signed with Mid-Southern Wrestling, which, at the time, was as close to the big leagues as one could get in wrestling without actually being in the big leagues. Mid-Southern Wrestling's roster included Jerry Lawler, who was already a star, as well as Rick Rude, Eddie Gilbert, and Jim

Neidhart, who were well on the way to becoming stars.

By that time, Randy had bulked up to a muscular 235 pounds. He was also billing himself as from Sarasota, Florida, where he had settled down during his minor league baseball career. Managed by Jimmy Hart, the colorful manager known as "The Mouth of the South" because of his loud, fast-talking ways, Randy quickly moved to the top of the federation and won several Mid-Southern championships. For the first time in his career, Randy was getting noticed. Several Lawler vs. Savage bouts attracted sellout crowds to the Mid-South Coliseum, where Lawler was the hometown hero.

One of Randy's matches, however, was conducted in a completely empty Mid-South Coliseum. It was a match against his brother, Lanny, with Lawler as referee. The match was held for the benefit of a wrestling magazine. Randy won.

Whether the match was held in front of an audience or an empty arena, it didn't matter. The word was out: Savage was a star in the making, a competitor to watch.

His final Mid-Southern title reign started on May 16, 1985, when he beat Jerry Oske, and ended on June 3, 1985, when he lost the title to Lawler. Randy never asked for a rematch. He never wanted one.

Shortly afterward, he left Mid-Southern Wrestling and signed with the WWF. After 12 years of paying his dues, Randy finally had his big break. For the first time in his life, he was a major leaguer.

3

A LADY NAMED ELIZABETH

Here's something most people don't know, and Randy Savage never wanted you to know. On December 30, 1984, Randy Mario Poffo married Elizabeth Ann Hulette in Franklin County, Kentucky. The groom was 32 years old. The bride was 24. The witnesses were Mary Ann Hulette, the bride's mother, and Paul Christy, the groom's friend and occasional opponent.

Randy Mario Poffo was, of course, Randy Savage.

Elizabeth Ann Hulette would one day become known to the wrestling world as Miss Elizabeth, or, simply, Elizabeth, the First Lady of Wrestling.

They had met several years earlier, when Randy was wrestling and Elizabeth was announcing in ICW. But in 1985, when Randy arrived in the WWF, few people knew he was married, and he wanted to keep it that way.

Savage's arrival in the WWF came at a time when Hulk Hogan had become the dominant figure in wrestling. Hogan had won the WWF World title from the Iron Sheik in early 1984 and wasted no time becoming not only the most popular wrestler in the world, but one of the most recognized faces in all of sports. Wrestling had become more colorful, with outrageous individuals wearing outrageous outfits and doing out-

After signing with the WWF in 1985, Savage started wearing cowboy hats and calling himself the Macho Man.

rageous things. Glitz and glamour had become the name of the game.

Savage fit right in. His long, wild hair, colorful headbands and wrestling tights, and intense eyes gave him the look of a madman. He gave rambling, wide-ranging interviews, his voice sounding strange as he spoke through gritted teeth and growled, "Ooooooh, yeah!" He gave himself a colorful nickname: the Macho Man.

An intelligent man attuned to the ways of the game, Savage recognized what having a manager in the Mid-Southern area had done for his career. So when he arrived in the WWF, he started looking for a new manager. There were numerous candidates and a wild bidding war ensued for his services. Experienced hands such as Mr. Fuji, Bobby Heenan, Fred Blassie, Johnny Valiant, and even Jimmy Hart tried to get into Savage's good graces. Many people felt Hart had the inside edge because of his previous experience managing Savage in Memphis, but one relatively unknown candidate had the biggest inside edge of all.

Savage wanted to make people think there was a bidding war for his services, but the truth was that he had already made his decision: Elizabeth would be his manager. The decision shocked the wrestling world because so few people knew of her managerial abilities, and fewer still knew they were married.

In addition to being the Macho Man's wife, Elizabeth had two more things going for her: she was smart and she was beautiful. She had long, wavy brown hair, sparkling brown eyes, high cheekbones that a model would envy, and a pixyish smile. She was the girl next door, the girl any man would have loved to bring home to mother, and any mother would have loved to have her son bring home. She was nothing like today's bombastic blondes of wrestling.

"A beautiful woman complements me," Savage explained. "She's a reflection of me, so it's right for her to be my manager."

It was hard to see the reflection. Elizabeth was demure and polite. Savage . . . . well, he was a savage rulebreaker. He was verbally abusive to her and often threatened to use physical force to make her do as he pleased. He'd make her hold down the ring ropes for him to make his entrance. She was more like his valet than his manager and she attended to his every need. Publicly, she rarely spoke. Because of Savage's treatment of Elizabeth, he was hated by the fans, while she became a favorite, especially of male fans.

Behind the scenes, however, Elizabeth would be the driving force behind Savage's success. She really wasn't a strategist as much as she was a brilliant business manager and an inspirational presence. Elizabeth convinced Savage to go after the WWF Intercontinental title, then held by Tito Santana. She figured that winning the title would put him in position to get shots at Hogan, the World champion.

Savage became wanton in his disregard for the rules. A prime example of this was his performance in a tournament at the Wrestling Classic, the WWF's first-ever pay-per-view event, held on November 7, 1985. In the first round, Savage illegally used the ropes for leverage to pin Ivan Putski. In the second round, Savage knocked out Rick Steamboat with a pair of brass knuckles, then scored the pin. Savage pinned Dynamite Kid in the semifinals, then lost to Junkyard Dog by countout in the championship.

With his manic style and mistreatment of Elizabeth, Savage had become one of the most feared rulebreakers in the world. He was ruthless and ferocious. On February 7, 1986, less than a year after his arrival in the WWF, Savage defeated Tito Santana to capture the Intercontinental title.

Savage's victory led to an unusual feud with George "the Animal" Steele. The Animal was an offbeat competitor. He had a round, bald head, beady eyes, and a green tongue. He rarely spoke; he grunted. He carried around a "pet" turnbuckle that he caressed lovingly. The Animal seemingly had the brain of an animal, but he was like a human being in at least one way: he had the ability to love.

In a real-life reenactment of the story of *Beauty and the Beast*, Steele developed a crush on Elizabeth and began bringing her flowers while she was at ringside for Savage's matches. Elizabeth, who had been so mistreated by Savage, seemed to enjoy Steele's attention. Not surprisingly, this made Savage intensely jealous, and he concentrated his efforts on destroying his challenger for Elizabeth's heart.

Savage defeated Steele at WrestleMania II on April 7, 1986, then engaged in a lengthy feud with the Animal. One time, Steele actually picked up Elizabeth and carried her backstage. Savage, enraged, chased after Steele and beat him up.

The feud struck a nerve with wrestling fans. Steele's affection for Elizabeth was sweet, if not misguided. He saw her as a beautiful creature to be loved and protected, while Savage treated

Elizabeth like a possession. Elizabeth was quoted as calling Savage "the meanest man I know." But, she hoped out loud, "maybe he won't be mean forever."

Instead, Savage became meaner. Rick Steamboat, an outstanding scientific wrestler, paid the price for targeting the Intercontinental title. One night, Savage brutalized Steamboat with the timekeeper's bell. He didn't care that he got disqualified; in the WWF, a champion can lose the title only by getting pinned or submitting. Savage had no intention of submitting to anybody, and he enjoyed brutalizing Steamboat without having to worry about losing the belt.

Elizabeth was Randy Savage's manager, valet, and wife, but the two kept their marriage a secret from the wrestling world.

Savage and Steamboat feuded throughout the winter of 1986 and into 1987. Steamboat was enormously popular and Savage was becoming more hated by the day. Their feud culminated at WrestleMania III on March 29, 1987, in Pontiac, Michigan. That day, the Silverdome was packed with more than 93,000 fans. They had come to watch Hogan battle Andre the Giant in the main event, but Steamboat and Savage nearly stole the show. In a classic match, during which the advantage changed hands several times and both men scored numerous near-pins, Steamboat needed 14 minutes, 35 seconds to pin the Macho Man for the title.

Savage immediately set his sights on regaining the title from Steamboat, but after two months of failure, something entirely unexpected happened: the Honky Tonk Man, who had been considered one of the WWF's most ridiculous wrestlers, shockingly upset Steamboat for the Intercontinental belt. The Honky Tonk Man was hated by the fans. He fancied himself a rock star, the reincarnation of Elvis Presley, and he liked to tell people, "I'm cool, I'm cocky, I'm bad!" He was, in a word, obnoxious.

This posed a problem for Savage. Back in the 1980s, the distinction between good and evil, between fan favorites and rulebreakers, was clearly drawn. Because of this, wrestling promoters never allowed fan favorites to wrestle other fan favorites, or rulebreakers to wrestler other rulebreakers, especially when a title was on the line. Wrestling was always a war between good and evil.

But if the Honky Tonk Man was a rulebreaker, that meant Savage, another rulebreaker, would never get the chance to wrestle him for the Intercontinental title.

Fortunately for Savage, he had Elizabeth on his side. The fans already loved her. Now all he had to do was undergo a bit of an image change, soften up, and make it so the fans liked him, too. Well, for Savage, changing his image to that of a fan favorite was as simple as starting a feud with the Honky Tonk Man.

Savage's popularity skyrocketed. By the end of 1987, he was the number two drawing card in the WWF, trailing only Hogan in fan appeal. Although nobody knew they were already married, Elizabeth and Savage became wrestling's First Couple.

An unusual series of events led to Savage's biggest break of all. The feud between Andre the Giant and Hogan culminated in a match on February 5, 1988, in Indianapolis, Indiana. The match was aired on NBC-TV, marking wrestling's return to prime-time network TV after a 33-year absence, and the evening had all the drama of a daytime soap opera.

Andre scored a controversial pinfall when an imposter referee made the count, even though Hogan's shoulder had lifted before the count of three. Less than two minutes later, Andre handed the belt to his manager, Ted DiBiase.

The next day, WWF president Jack Tunney ruled the exchange invalid and decided that by giving DiBiase the belt, Andre had forfeited the title. He ordered a tournament for the World title to be held at WrestleMania IV.

Fourteen of the WWF's top wrestlers entered the tournament, which was held on March 27, 1988, at the Atlantic City Convention Center. Hogan and Andre received first-round byes, then met in the second round and battled to a double-disqualification. As a result, both men were eliminated from the tournament.

Savage fared much better. He pinned Butch Reed in the first round. In the second round, he pinned Greg Valentine. In the semifinals, Savage beat the huge One Man Gang by dis-qualification.

Savage was one victory away from achieving his goal. His opponent in the championship match was DiBiase, who, having failed to buy the belt, now wanted to win it in the traditional manner.

But there was nothing traditional about this match. The sellout crowd at the Convention Center roared as Savage and Elizabeth made their way to the ring. Elizabeth looked beautiful. She wore a white, shoulderless cocktail dress and sparkling crystal earrings. There was

Savage, Elizabeth, and Hulk Hogan face the press following the Macho Man's victory over Ted DiBiase at Wrestlemania IV on March 27, 1988, in Atlantic City. Savage beat three contenders en route to the title match with DiBiase, and with a little help from Hogan, he was able to secure his first WWF championship.

no doubt whom the fans were rooting for, especially when Andre the Giant joined DiBiase in his corner.

With Andre on his side, there seemed to be no way DiBiase could lose, until the great equalizer made his entrance midway through the match. The great equalizer was Hogan, and when he ran down the runway to the ring, the entire crowd stood and roared its approval.

It was a dramatic moment in wrestling history, an instant when worlds collided and nothing would ever be the same again. Hogan stood with Elizabeth at ringside and rooted on Savage. In the opposite corner, Andre glared angrily at the "Hulkster." With a little over nine minutes gone, DiBiase caught Savage in a headlock, while referee Dave Hebner argued with Andre.

Hogan seized the advantage. He grabbed a folding chair, bounded into the ring, and smacked DiBiase across the back. Hogan escaped from the ring as Hebner turned back to the action and Savage mounted the turn-buckle. The Macho Man got ready, aimed, and fired. He came down with a flying elbowsmash, his favorite finishing maneuver, and nailed DiBiase. A three-count later, Savage was the new WWF World champion.

What a glorious moment! Hogan and Eliza-beth bounded back into the ring to celebrate. The crowd erupted with applause. Hogan and Savage shook hands, then Savage hoisted Elizabeth onto his shoulders. With Elizabeth proudly holding the WWF World championship belt, Savage paraded his beautiful manager around the ring.

They were the king and queen of the WWF.

And Hogan's contribution to the victory was not to be forgotten. Hogan and Savage were about to make wrestling history as the Megapowers.

4 THE ROYAL WEDDING

Jealousy is an evil emotion. It has destroyed friendships and ripped families apart. It is a product of egotism, which both Randy Savage and Hulk Hogan had in abundance. It is also a product of insecurity, which perhaps both Savage and Hogan tried to hide behind their career accomplishments.

On the surface, the Megapowers didn't seem to have a chance. Savage was the WWF World champion, a title Hogan had held for over four years, and dearly wanted to win again. Could Hogan, the most famous wrestler ever, handle being number two to anyone, particularly his tag team partner?

What about Savage? Had he really changed so much since two years earlier, when he had become enraged by George Steele's wooing of Elizabeth? Had he really become less jealous? Could Savage stand sharing Elizabeth's attention with Hogan?

For a while, all was fine. The Megapowers grew closer after a brutal attack by DiBiase and Andre the Giant. While a worldwide television audience watched, Andre attacked Savage while DiBiase held Elizabeth. That led to a showdown at SummerSlam '88, in which Hogan and Savage teamed to beat DiBiase and Andre in one of the most anticipated matches of the year. Savage pinned DiBiase in 13 minutes, 57 seconds at

---

Randy Savage squeezes Hulk Hogan, his one-time tag team partner, in a headlock. Savage and Hogan were the Megapowers until jealousy over Elizabeth tore them apart.

Madison Square Garden in New York, and when it was over, Hogan and Savage both hoisted Elizabeth onto their shoulders. The Megapowers were the hottest thing going.

At the 1988 Survivor Series, a team consisting of Hogan, Savage, Koko B. Ware, Hillbilly Jim, and Hercules Hernandez defeated DiBiase and four others. The crowd was squarely behind the Megapowers, who didn't seem to be have any problems at all in getting along.

The alliance, however, was doomed to disaster from the start. These two men with their huge egos couldn't get along for long.

For the most part, the problem was Savage. Hogan couldn't look at Elizabeth or talk to her without Savage getting insanely jealous.

The end came on February 3, 1989, when the Megapowers battled Akeem and Big Bossman in a nationally televised card on NBC. Late in the match, Savage was thrown from the ring onto Elizabeth, knocking her unconscious. Hogan didn't know what to do. Both Elizabeth and Savage had been knocked out. His decision was fateful: he scooped up Elizabeth in his arms and carried her back to the dressing room.

Savage recovered, returned to the ring, and went on to defeat Akeem and Big Bossman, but winning didn't make him any happier. When he got back to the dressing room, he shoved Elizabeth, then attacked Hogan, knocking him to the floor several times.

The Megapowers had collapsed on national TV.

There was no doubt who the fans were going to side with in this feud. Once again, Savage was a rulebreaker. The question was, whose side was Elizabeth on?

The answer came at WrestleMania V on April 2, 1989, again in Atlantic City. On the line was Savage's WWF World heavyweight title . . . and the managerial services of Elizabeth.

It took Savage only 17 minutes, 54 seconds, to lose the two things that were dearest to him. Hogan was not only the World champion, but he had Miss Elizabeth, too.

As much of a rulebreaker as Savage had been before, and as mean and violent, he was about to become even more heartless. He found a new manager, "Sensational" Sherri Martel, a former World women's champion who was the opposite of Elizabeth in every way possible. She was heavy on the makeup, heavy on the talk, and heavy on any person, man or woman, who dared cross her path.

While never losing sight of Elizabeth, Savage set his sights on some new goals. He won the 1989 King of the Ring tournament and started calling himself the "Macho King." He continued his feud with Hogan. At SummerSlam '89, Savage and Zeus—the villain to Hogan's hero in the movie *No Holds Barred*—lost to Hogan and Brutus Beefcake. A month later, Hogan pinned Savage in Washington, D.C. Afterward, Hogan held Savage as Elizabeth slapped him. Then Hogan held Sherri and Elizabeth slapped her, too!

Savage's reputation took a nosedive. The losses piled up. As his feud with Hogan became more lopsided, Savage stopped getting title shots. And the whispers started. People were talking. The fact that Savage's career had gone nowhere before Elizabeth and was going nowhere after Elizabeth was too much of a coincidence to ignore. For a man with an ego as large as Savage's, the accusations that he was nothing without Elizabeth were hard to take.

Perhaps Savage's lowest point came at the nationally televised Main Event on February 23, 1990, in Detroit. James "Buster" Douglas, who had beaten Mike Tyson 12 days earlier for the boxing heavyweight title, was special referee for a match between Hogan and Savage. Again Hogan won, connecting with a legdrop to score the pin. Savage, however, was incensed by what he thought was a fast count. He argued with Douglas and pranced around the ring like

After losing Elizabeth to Hulk Hogan, Savage hired "Sensational" Sherri Martel, right, to be his new manager. Before long however, Sherri Martel would turn her back on Savage.

he wanted to box. Savage slapped Douglas in the face, but the boxer refused to react. When Savage incited him further, Douglas delivered two big rights, knocking Savage to the canvas.

A month later at WrestleMania VI, Savage and Sherri lost to Rhodes and Sapphire in the WWF's first-ever mixed tag team match. On the same card, the Ultimate Warrior pinned Hogan for the World title. The Megapowers had fallen, but nobody had fallen further than Savage.

Savage did little but complain about his situation. He called the Ultimate Warrior a coward for not granting him enough World title shots. The Warrior answered the challenge and soundly defeated Savage several times. In one particularly embarrassing performance, Savage rolled out of the ring and ran back to the safety of his dressing room. Warrior caught up with Savage, threw him into the ring, then belted him with three clotheslines and a flying tackle. Battered and bruised, Savage ran from the ring and used Sherri to shield him from the Warrior. This time, the Warrior let him run back to the dressing room.

Incredibly, Savage had the nerve to suggest that the Warrior was ducking him! At the 1991 Royal Rumble, Savage and Sherri interfered in the Warrior's title defense against Sergeant Slaughter. Savage's attack on the Warrior cost him the World title and led to a showdown at WrestleMania VII.

The Savage-Warrior showdown at Wrestle-Mania was a retirement match. The loser would have to hang up his tights for good. Savage didn't stand a chance. The Warrior was intent on ending the Macho Man's career. Sherri interfered, but her interference backfired. When she leaped off the top rope to hit Warrior with her shoe, he moved and she struck Savage instead. When Warrior went after her, Savage snuck up from behind and rolled him up for a two-count.

It was a great bout. Savage and the Warrior battled for over 20 minutes, with the advantage changing hands several times. Indeed, it was the best Savage had ever wrestled against the Warrior. The match turned on a bad break for Savage: Warrior moved out of the way of Savage's attempted flying axhandle and Savage smashed into the ring railing. Warrior knocked out Savage with a shouldertackle, then scored the pin.

The loss brought out the worst in Sherri, who kicked at Savage repeatedly. She was bitter and didn't want to be associated with a loser, especially a retired loser. Suddenly, Elizabeth emerged from the crowd and threw Sherri out of the ring.

The fans were exultant! If it was possible for a man to change from rulebreaker to fan favorite in a split-second, it had happened before their eyes. Savage got up and stared at Elizabeth in disbelief. They embraced. Fans at ringside actually cried. Savage hoisted her on his shoulders and carried her around the ring. Then he held the ropes for her as they left the ring together.

It was a bittersweet moment. Despite this emotional conclusion to a great match, Savage had lost. And that meant he had to retire.

But he didn't disappear. Savage continued to do interviews and provide commentary on WWF TV. The WWF allowed him to fulfill his remaining wrestling commitments. The fans viewed another shocking change of attitude as

Savage turned into an emotional softie. He expressed his love for Elizabeth. He asked the fans if he should propose to her, and they agreed that he should. He proposed to her on TV. Of course, he and Elizabeth were already married, but the fans didn't know that.

In 1991, Savage was finally ready to let the world know that he loved Elizabeth and that she felt the same way. Wrestling's version of the Royal Wedding took place at SummerSlam '91 on August 26 at Madison Square Garden in New York City. The groom was handsome. The bride was beautiful. There were more than 20,000 witnesses. The wedding went off without a hitch. Even WWF announcer Gene Okerlund shed a tear.

The wedding reception, however, was another story. The Undertaker and Jake "The Snake" Roberts showed up uninvited. Roberts handed Elizabeth a gift. She opened it. To her horror, inside was a dangerous snake.

This traumatizing event sent Elizabeth into a state of depression. Fans petitioned WWF President Jack Tunney to reinstate Savage so he could get revenge against The Undertaker and Roberts.

At first, Tunney refused to reinstate Savage, but when Roberts allowed his pet snake to bite Savage, the WWF President had little choice but to allow the Macho Man back into the ring.

With Elizabeth by his side.

5 CAN'T KEEP A "MACHO MAN" DOWN

The shocking footage of Jake Roberts's snake biting Randy Savage on the arm was played over and over on WWF broadcasts. One concession was made to the viewing public, as the actual bite was optically censored to protect the squeamish.

After getting bitten by the venomous snake, Savage was rushed away on a stretcher and quickly treated by medical personnel. Roberts was suspended from the Survivor Series and the reptile was banned from all future matches—not that he should have been there in the first place.

Savage and Roberts finally had their showdown on December 4, 1991, in San Antonio, Texas, and Roberts spent most of the match attacking Savage's heavily bandaged right arm. Roberts partially unwrapped the bandage, but the Macho Man was relentless in his attack, finally pinning Roberts after a flying elbowsmash from the top turnbuckle.

But the encounter didn't end there. Savage grabbed the ring bell and went after Roberts, but the Snake got up and knocked him out with a series of crushing blows. With Savage unconscious, Roberts reached under the apron, pulled out a black bag, and brought it into the ring. Was a snake inside the bag? Elizabeth, crying and whimpering, perhaps fearing for

---

After winning the WWF title from Ric Flair in 1992, Savage's world seemed to fall apart: his marriage to Elizabeth ended in divorce, his legs were injured, and he lost the WWF title back to Flair. Still, the 40-year-old Savage refused to give up.

her life, ran into the ring and threw her body over Savage's. Roberts taunted Savage and Elizabeth, then threatened Elizabeth, but WWF officials intervened and nobody ever found out what, if anything, was in the bag.

The feud continued with Savage and Hacksaw Duggan teaming against Roberts and The Undertaker and beating them most of the time. Once again, however, Savage had trapped himself in a relatively meaningless feud, and his World title prospects were slipping away. When 1992 started, two years and eight months had passed since Savage last wore the WWF World championship belt.

At the time, the WWF title was in turmoil. WWF president Jack Tunney had declared the

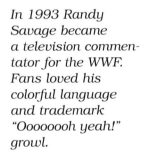

In 1993 Randy Savage became a television commentator for the WWF. Fans loved his colorful language and trademark "Oooooooh yeah!" growl.

belt vacant as the result of a controversy
between Hulk Hogan and The Undertaker.
Tunney put the belt up for grabs at the 1992
Royal Rumble. Savage was one of the last four
men remaining, but he was eliminated by Flair,
who went on to win the match and the title.

The ruthless Flair immediately set his sights
on Savage. He announced that he had had a
relationship with Elizabeth several years earlier
and produced photos of the two of them together.
When Savage stepped into the ring against Flair
at WrestleMania VIII, he was as intent on
destroying Flair as he was on regaining the
World title.

This time, Savage's insane jealousy worked
to his advantage. He wrestled like a man possessed, bloodied Flair, and scored the pin at
18:05. Not only had he protected Elizabeth's
honor, but he had won his second World title.

Even Flair couldn't have known how
painfully he had struck a nerve with Savage.
Flaunting a relationship with Elizabeth, whether
or not it actually ever happened, was exactly
the wrong tactic to take at the time. Savage and
Elizabeth's seven-year marriage was coming to
an end. Soon they would be divorced. As far as
the public knew, their marriage had lasted less
than a year.

"While I was wrestling on the road, I would
call home and there was no answer for four
days and Elizabeth was M.I.A.—missing in
action—for four days," Savage explained years
later. "I was worried about my wife then, and I
still am now. I can't help that, because in my
heart, I'll always love her. It's very hard to let
go, but you've got to let go. Four days went by
and Liz called me and told me to get a lawyer

because she wanted a divorce. That was the end of the story right there."

Elizabeth stopped coming to the ring for Savage's matches, and the Macho Man started looking for a new manager. Coincidentally, both he and the Ultimate Warrior settled on Curt Hennig, a former AWA World champion. Unfortunately for Savage, Hennig hadn't settled on him. During the Savage–Warrior showdown at SummerSlam '92, both Hennig and Flair came to the ring and interfered on the Warrior's behalf. After Flair blasted him with a chair, Savage was counted out. He had lost and he was badly injured.

Three days later in Hershey, Pennsylvania, Savage limped to the ring for a match against Flair. His leg had been battered by Flair and Hennig at SummerSlam, but he had no choice but to wrestle. This time, Flair got help from Hennig, Bobby Heenan, and Razor Ramon. The Macho Man tried to walk back to the dressing room, but his legs collapsed beneath him. He had to be carried back by the Warrior.

Distraught over losing Elizabeth and wrestling on one good leg, Savage couldn't regain the title. He teamed with the Ultimate Warrior, but they failed in several attempts to win the World tag team title. Life had hit rock bottom for the Macho Man.

He tried to get his career back on track, but nothing went right. The old anger, the old killer instinct, just wasn't enough. Ramon humbled Savage. Flair humbled Savage. Savage actually teamed with Hennig against Ramon and Flair at the 1992 Survivor Series, and the unlikely duo won the match, but Savage's career continued its downhill slide.

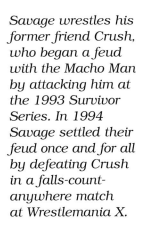

*Savage wrestles his
former friend Crush,
who began a feud
with the Macho Man
by attacking him at
the 1993 Survivor
Series. In 1994
Savage settled their
feud once and for all
by defeating Crush
in a falls-count-
anywhere match
at Wrestlemania X.*

After nearly winning the Royal Rumble on January 24, 1993, Savage decided to take a breather. Although he occasionally wrestled, he mostly concentrated on his new career as a TV commentator. He did TV commercials for Slim Jim snacks and became active in fund-raising for the Special Olympics and the Leukemia Society. Savage's face was more recognized than ever before, but his career progress didn't match his upturn in popularity.

Why the slowdown? Well, let's place Savage's career in perspective. Although WWF fans had known him only since 1985, he had been an

*Randy Savage has
fun with some of
his friends during
a fund-raiser for the
Special Olympics.*

active wrestler for 19 years. The previous
November, he had turned 40 years old. His legs
were battered. For the past seven years, he had
wrestled an extremely ambitious schedule. His
marriage was over. He didn't have a manager.
His prospects of regaining the belt were slim.

The Macho Man's life was at a crossroads,
and he wasn't making a move in any direction.

Not that he had lost his touch in the ring.
When he did wrestle, he looked fine. For example, he defeated Intercontinental champion
Shawn Michaels by disqualification, but failed
to win the belt because a champion can lose his

title only by submission or pinfall. He occasionally snuck into the WWF Top 10. He teamed with Crush. His TV commentary was colorful and entertaining, so his popularity grew. Fans wanted to hear what he had to say, even if they couldn't always understand what he had to say. Every other maniacally delivered sentence was punctuated by a growl of "Ooooooh yeah!"

Then, in October, Savage stepped back in time to his roots in Memphis, Tennessee. When WWF owner Vince McMahon ignited a war between the WWF and the United States Wrestling Alliance (USWA), Savage went to Memphis to fight on the WWF's behalf. Representing the USWA was Jerry Lawler, Savage's rival from his Mid-Southern days. On October 11, 1993, Savage benefited from McMahon's interference and won the USWA heavyweight title. Savage, however, failed to defend the title even once and was soon stripped of the belt.

Times were changing. As 1994 began, the wrestling world was on the verge of a vast upheaval. The WWF was losing fan support. Its image was taking a beating. McMahon was indicted by a federal grand jury (he would later be acquitted) on charges of dealing in steroids. Bobby Heenan, the controversial but popular WWF commentator, left for World Championship Wrestling (WCW). Since 1984, when Hogan had arrived in the federation, the WWF had been the dominant wrestling organization in North America. Ted Turner, the billionaire cable TV magnate who owned WCW, was about to dip into his deep pockets and make the battle a little more even.

Savage's final WWF feud was against Crush, a fellow wrestler and former friend. Crush accused Savage of turning his back on him when he was injured, and tried to gain revenge by attacking him at the 1993 Survivor Series. The feud, one of the most heated of 1994, culminated at WrestleMania X with a falls-count-anywhere match. In an unusual finish, Savage tied up Crush in a secluded room in the bowels of Madison Square Garden. Crush couldn't get back to the ring within 60 seconds and Savage was awarded the victory.

After the feud with Crush, Savage never seemed focused in the WWF. He competed occasionally in Smoky Mountain Wrestling and renewed his rivalry with Jake Roberts. Sometimes he wrestled in the WWF. Sometimes he did TV commentary. He was split between two careers.

Then Ted Turner dropped the first bomb in his war against the WWF: on June 11, 1994, WCW signed Hulk Hogan. The wrestler whose name was synonymous with the WWF was now working for the competition.

Five months later, Savage reached the end of his WWF run, too.

Ironically, Savage's departure from the WWF came just weeks after he had pledged allegiance to the federation. Interviewed for a cover story in *WWF Magazine*, Savage vowed, "I don't care if Joe's Bar and Grill and a guy named Huber have got 40 million dollars in cash to give me. The big league is the World Wrestling Federation. Just like in the NBA, you don't go to the CBA just because they pay you more money. I'm in a position where money isn't a factor."

On November 7, during a live broadcast of *Monday Night Raw*, McMahon announced that

the WWF had been unable to come to terms
with the Macho Man on a new contract.

"I had some great times in the WWF,"
Savage said. "I'm leaving on the best of terms. I
have a lot of friends there, and I want to thank
the WWF for all they have done for me. I'd also
like to thank my fans for all their support over
the years. You never know where the Macho
Man will show up next."

It didn't take long to find out. On December
3, 1994, Savage appeared on a live broadcast of
WCW Saturday Night. He told the world that he
had come to WCW to confront Hogan.

"I've still got some unfinished business with
the man," Savage warned.

As rumors circulated that Elizabeth, too,
would show up in WCW, the wrestling world
braced for another showdown between the
Megapowers.

BORN AGAIN

At the same time that Savage made his WCW debut, the issue of *WWF Magazine* in which he declared his allegiance to the WWF appeared on the newsstands. To some, it might have seemed as if there were two Randy "Macho Man" Savages walking the earth, each acting contrarily to the other. Anyone who had closely followed his career knew that it always seemed that way.

So when Savage announced that he would either slap Hogan's face or shake his hand at Starrcade '94, nobody was sure what he was going to do. The smart money, however, was on Savage slapping his face.

If there was any doubt, all anybody had to do was refer back to an interview Savage gave to WWF Radio back in 1993.

"I personally used to look up to Hulk Hogan, but that was a big mistake," Savage said. "I really thought he was a friend, but he's definitely not. He's the worst prima donna I've ever met in my life."

Savage then went on to accuse Hogan of breaking up his marriage to Elizabeth, and he even implied that Hogan and Elizabeth had a relationship. Indeed, shaking Hogan's hand looked like an unlikely option for Savage. Then again, this was the Macho Man. The unpredictable Macho Man.

Savage left the WWF for WCW in 1994 and made his return to the wrestling ring, winning his first WCW World heavyweight title at a 60-man battle royal on November 26, 1995.

Savage poses for the camera at the Great American Bash in Baltimore on June 14, 1998. One day later, NWO Hollywood attacked Savage, breaking his leg and sidelining him into 1999.

At Starrcade, Avalanche and Kevin Sullivan attacked Hogan. Savage ran out to the ring . . . and he shook Hogan's hand.

In the weeks that followed, Savage made a full-fledged return to the ring. He looked good. The old killer instinct had returned. Maybe all he needed was a change of scenery.

Of course, the scenery hadn't really changed that much. The federation was different, but a lot of the names were the same. Hogan. Brutus Beefcake. And Ric Flair.

Flair, disguised in women's clothing and a wig, attacked Savage at the Uncensored pay-per-view on March 19, 1995, renewing the feud from their WWF days. Obviously, neither man had forgotten the other.

The Megapowers reunited to battle Flair and Big Van Vader at Slamboree '95. It was going to be a happy night for Savage: Angelo Poffo would be inducted into the WCW Hall of Fame, and then watch from a ringside seat while his son wrestled.

It turned into a night of horrors.

Hogan and Flair had just won the match when Flair and Vader decided to relieve their frustrations. Vader, Flair, and Arn Anderson unleashed a three-way assault on Savage. Poffo, who was sitting at ringside, climbed over the metal ring barrier and rushed to assist his fallen son. What happened next was almost unspeakable: Vader and Flair pummeled the 70-year-old man, then Flair trapped him in a figure-four leglock, injuring his leg.

Outraged over the incident, Savage demanded that WCW suspend Flair.

"He's madder than I've seen anyone," Hogan said of Savage. "Just imagine, he was right there when those animals attacked his father. We always knew those guys had no respect for anyone, but this time they went too far."

Said Savage: "Put all three of them in a cage with me, I don't care. I don't care if I win or if I lose. This isn't about winning or losing, this is about revenge. It's about getting even. You know what, brother? It's about duty."

He was right about that, although revenge wouldn't come until many months later.

The WCW World title, which had been declared vacant in October, was put up for grabs in a 60-man battle royal at the World War III pay-per-view on November 26, 1995. After

29 minutes and 19 seconds, Savage was the only man left in the ring. He had won his first WCW World heavyweight title.

But the victory was not without controversy. Hogan claimed that he had not been eliminated, but had been pulled underneath the bottom rope by The Giant.

"There is a dark cloud over your title," Hogan told Savage. "You didn't go over the top, and I didn't go over the top."

Hogan was incensed when WCW officials didn't overturn the decision and Savage didn't offer to give back the belt. The controversy didn't last long, however, because on December 27 at Starrcade '95, Flair beat Savage for the title.

And less than a month later, on January 23, 1996, Savage regained the title from Flair.

Winning the WCW World title twice in a month was an amazing achievement for a man who, just a year ago, was considering retirement.

Things were going well for Savage until a new distraction arrived on the scene. His ex-wife and manager, Elizabeth, had signed with WCW and was back in his corner. But was Elizabeth by his side or getting ready to stab him in the back?

On February 11, 1996, Savage stepped into the ring at SuperBrawl VI to defend his title in a steel cage match against Flair. Elizabeth was in Savage's corner. Just when the Macho Man appeared to be in control of the match, Elizabeth handed Flair one of her high-heeled shoes. Flair used the shoe to knock out Savage, score the pin, and regain the World title.

"I've been waiting to do that for a long time," Elizabeth said as she was ushered off to a private dressing room.

The worst was yet to come. In the spring of 1996, two former WWF stars, Diesel and Razor Ramon, invaded WCW under their real names, Kevin Nash and Scott Hall. They vowed to destroy WCW, and a match was signed pitting Savage, Luger, and Sting against Nash, Hall and a mystery partner at Bash at the Beach on July 7, 1996.

The match was a turning point in wrestling history. The mystery partner turned out to be Hogan, who entered the ring near the end of the match and legdropped a fallen Savage.

Hogan, Nash, Hall, and The Giant, along with WCW president Eric Bischoff and several wrestlers, formed the New World Order (NWO), a supergroup intent on controlling the federation from the inside. For the first time since the early 1980s, Hogan was a rulebreaker. The NWO would go on to become the most powerful clique in wrestling history.

Savage was their target. At a WCW *Monday Nitro* broadcast on September 2, 1996, The Giant choke-slammed Savage, then Hogan spray-painted a yellow streak down his back.

Randy Savage and Hulk Hogan stand with their friend Kevin Greene of the Pittsburgh Steelers, center, after Savage regained the WCW World title from Ric Flair at Clash of the Champions on January 23, 1996, in Las Vegas.

Savage waged a dangerous one-man war against the NWO; it was a losing battle. NWO members attacked him relentlessly, smashing him with chairs and tables.

"We've done the 'Macho Puke' a favor so far," Hogan said. "We've let him get up from our beatings. He's lucky we haven't crippled him yet."

Savage was an emotional wreck. He didn't know how to react when Elizabeth begged him for forgiveness. He wanted to forgive her, but he didn't know if he was going to be the victim of another ruse. Emotionally torn, Savage took a break from wrestling after losing to Hogan at Halloween Havoc '96.

Rumors circulated that Savage was returning to the WWF. Other rumors circulated that he had decided to forgive Elizabeth. Still another rumor circulated that Savage was entertaining an offer to join the NWO.

Savage didn't make his intentions clear when he returned to WCW in late January, but he left no doubts at SuperBrawl VII on February 23, 1997. Savage was at ringside, supposedly to root on WCW World champion Roddy Piper in his match against Hogan. Indeed, it was inconceivable that Savage could side with the NWO, the group that had caused him so much pain, and befriend Hogan, his archenemy.

But the inconceivable happened when Savage slipped a pair of brass knuckles to Hogan, who used them to beat Piper for the title.

"The NWO strikes again!" Hogan exclaimed.

Elizabeth was back with Savage, too, although nobody dared guess for how long. This time, however, Elizabeth wasn't the

beloved princess she used to be. She had hard-
ened over the years, and the fans now hated
her as much as they hated the Macho Man. She
was his partner in a violent NWO crime spree.

They were a heartless pair. No longer united
by love, they wreaked havoc. At the Uncensored
'97 pay-per-view in March, Savage and Elizabeth berated Kimberly, "Diamond" Dallas
Page's wife and valet, for posing in *Playboy*
magazine. Kimberly stumbled out from the
dressing room covered in spray paint. Page
tried to defend Kimberly, then got painted, too.

The feud intensified when Hogan and
Savage sneak-attacked Page and injured his
ribs. Scott Hall's interference allowed Savage to
pin Page at the Great American Bash in June.
The feud extended deep into the fall, effectively
preventing Savage from making a serious run
at a major title.

But there was trouble within the NWO.
Several NWO members, including Hogan,
started questioning Savage's loyalty and sanity.
They couldn't be blamed: Savage had attacked
other NWO members during tag team matches.

"The Macho Man marches to the beat of a
different drummer," Savage said. "I do what I
want when I want. If I want to elbowsmash
Kevin Nash, then I'll do it. It doesn't mean I'm
any less dedicated to the group, and in fact the
'Macho Man' personifies what the NWO is all
about: reckless abandon. I am NWO for life."

He wasn't, however, Hogan's friend for life.
He didn't want to quit the NWO. He didn't even
want to change the NWO. He merely wanted to
get rid of Hogan.

"My brothers in the New World Order are
tired of Savage's crap," Hogan proclaimed. "They

want to teach him a lesson that there is a pecking order, and there is no room for anarchy. We'll beat our philosophy of NWO 4 Life into the Macho Man one way or another, whether he likes it or not. Then he'll be shown the door."

He exited limping. Less than three weeks before he was to wrestle Sting for the World title at Spring Stampede on April 19, 1998, Savage tore the anterior cruciate ligament in his right knee. Six days later, he was brutally attacked by Hogan and suffered arm, neck, and shoulder injuries. Savage didn't know whether he'd be able to wrestle Sting. A few days before the match, however, he received clearance from doctors.

The match was violent and chaotic. Elizabeth interfered and got caught in the middle of a "Stinger splash." She had to be helped back to the dressing room. Hogan interfered and nearly cost Savage the match. Then Nash interfered, powerbombed Sting, and rolled Savage on top of him. Savage was a three-time WCW World champion.

Hogan was enraged. "That's my belt!" he shouted at Savage.

Indeed it was. The next night, Hogan benefited from interference by Bret Hart and pinned Savage for the title.

This series of events split the NWO in two. On one side was the Wolfpac, with Savage, Nash, and Sting. On the other side was NWO Hollywood, with Hogan, Bischoff, and Hall.

In the middle, as usual, was Elizabeth.

After all these years, Savage hadn't learned his lesson. He was still enraged when Elizabeth jumped to NWO Hollywood. He tried to act as though he didn't care, claiming, "I got over Liz a long time ago," but he sounded anything but convincing. And then there was a new wound: Savage was attacked by NWO Hollywood on June 15, 1998, and had his leg broken by Eric Bischoff.

The injury forced Savage to remain sidelined for the rest of 1998 and part of 1999, but if the past is any indication, his spirit hasn't been broken.

For the first 12 years of his wrestling career, Savage refused to give up fighting for his dream, even when he appeared to be getting nowhere. Since 1985, he has realized that dream and become a wrestling icon. He has appeared on television programs such as *Live with Regis and Kathy Lee*, *The Jeff Foxworthy Show*, and *Baywatch*. He is the only wrestler to have appeared on *Politically Incorrect*. His distinctive voice has landed him roles on the cartoons *Dial M for Monkey* and *Space Monkey*.

In February 1998, Savage was named *Harvard Lampoon*'s Real Man of the Year, which is given each year by editors of the Harvard University humor magazine to the male who best exemplifies universal manliness. Past winners included John Wayne, Billy Crystal, and Robin Williams.

There's no longer any doubt: does Randy "Macho Man" Savage belong on any list of the most famous and successful men in the world?

Ooooooh, yeah!

Chronology

1952 Born Randy Poffo in Columbus, Ohio, on November 15.

1973 Makes his pro wrestling debut in Clenbard, Illinois, and beats Paul Christy.

1984 Marries Elizabeth Ann Hulette, who later becomes his manager.

1985 Signs with the WWF.

1986 Beats Tito Santana for the WWF Intercontinental title.

1987 Loses the Intercontinental title to Rick Steamboat.

1988 Beats Ted DiBiase in a tournament final for his first WWF World heavyweight title.

1989 Loses the WWF World title to Hulk Hogan.
The Megapowers break up.

1991 Participates in wedding ceremony with Elizabeth at SummerSlam.

1992 Divorces Elizabeth.
Wins his second WWF World title from Ric Flair.
Loses the WWF World title to Ric Flair.

1994 Released from WWF contract by owner Vince McMahon.
Makes his WCW debut.

1995 Wins a 60-man battle royal for his first WCW World title.
Loses the WCW World title to Ric Flair.

1996 Beats Ric Flair for second WCW World title.
Loses the WCW World title to Ric Flair.

1998 Beats Sting for his third WCW World title.
Loses the WCW World title to Hulk Hogan.

1999 Loses the WCW championship to Kevin Nash in Baltimore.
Beats Kevin Nash in WCW championship match in Florida.
Beats Dennis Rodman at The Sturgis Rally and Races.

2000 Contract with WCW expires in January.
Rumored to be retired.

Further Reading

Anderson, Steve. "Deathwish! Costing Hogan the Title Isn't Enough for the "Macho Man" — What Next?" *The Wrestler* (July 1998): 34–37.

Murphy, Dan. "Savage's World (Dis)Order: Is Anyone Macho Enough to Stop the Madness?" *The Wrestler* (August 1998): 34–37.

Ricciuti, Edward R. *Face to Face with "Macho Man" Randy Savage.* Woodbridge, CT: Blackbirch Press, 1994.

Rosenbaum, Dave. "Referee's Report: 'I've Never Seen Pain Like I Saw in Savage's Face.' " *The Wrestler* (October 1998): 42–45.

"Q & A: Randy Savage." *The Wrestler* (June 1998): 20–23.

Index

Photo Credits

Associated Press/Wide World Photos: pp. 32, 46, 55; Jeff Eisenberg Sports Photography: pp. 2,
6, 8, 11, 18, 22, 30, 36, 40, 42, 45, 50, 60; Tampa Tribune: pp. 14, 17; WCW: pp. 27, 52.

JACQUELINE MUDGE is a frequent contributor to sports and entertainment magazines in the United States. Born in Idaho, she became a wrestling fan at age 11 when her father took her to matches. Although she has a degree in journalism, she left the writing arena for several years in the late-1980s to pursue a career in advertising sales. She returned to the profession—and the sport she loves—in 1995, and is now a correspondent for wrestling magazines around the world.